Simple Machines

Levers

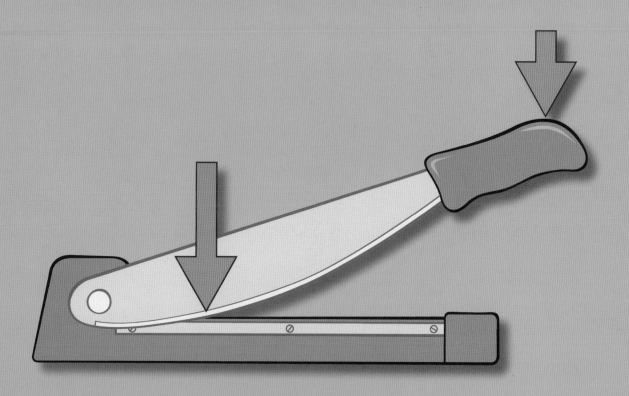

Chris Oxlade

A⁺
Smart Apple Media

Published by Smart Apple Media
2140 Howard Drive West
North Mankato, MN 56003

Designed by Helen James
Edited by Mary-Jane Wilkins
Artwork by Bill Donohoe

Photographs by
page 5 Lito C. Uyan/Corbis; 6 Gaetano/Corbis; 9 Colin Garratt; Milepost 92 1/2/Corbis;
11 Ole Graf/Zefa/Corbis; 12 First Light/Corbis; 15 Roy McMahon/Corbis; 18 Jeremy
Hardie/Zefa/Corbis; 19 Roy McMahon/Corbis; 20 Robert Llewellyn/Zefa/Corbis;
21 Courtesy of Hunter Engineering Company; 22 Enzo & Paolo Ragazzini/Corbis;
26 Patrick Johns/Corbis; 28 Mika/Zefa/Corbis

Printed in China

Library of Congress Cataloging-in-Publication Data

Oxlade, Chris.
Levers / by Chris Oxlade.
p. cm. — (Simple machines)
Includes index.
ISBN 978-1-59920-083-5
1. Levers—Juvenile literature. 2. Lifting and carrying—Juvenile !iterature.
3. Simple machines—Juvenile literature. I. Title.

TJ147.O84 2007
621.8—dc22   2007004879

First Edition

9 8 7 6 5 4 3 2 1

Contents

What is a simple machine?

A simple machine is something that helps you do a job. We use simple machines to help us every day. Here are some simple machines you might have at home.

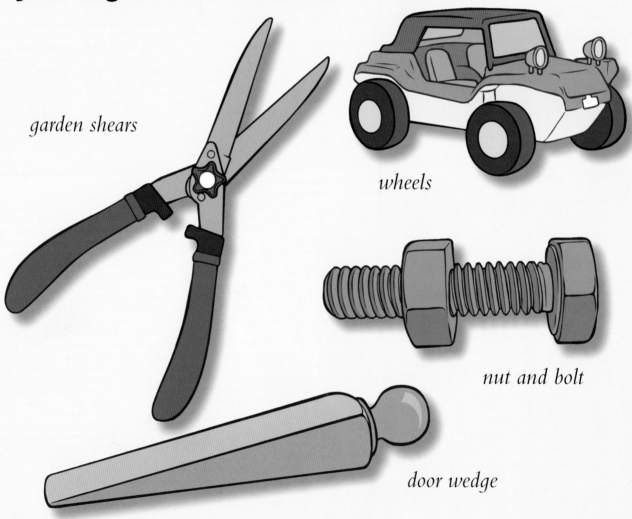

garden shears

wheels

nut and bolt

door wedge

4

This book is about simple machines called levers. A bottle opener is a lever. The opener makes it easier to pull off a metal bottle top. Door handles, scissors, wrenches, and nut crackers are all levers.

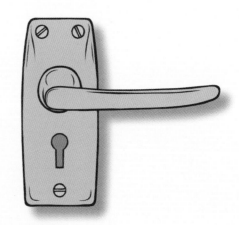

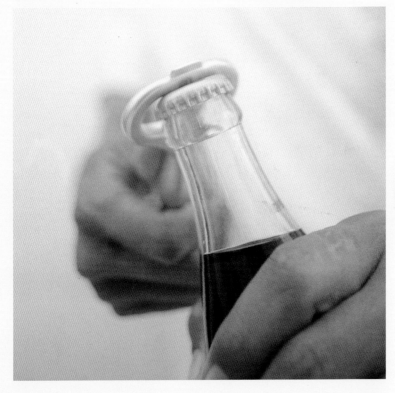

Pulling up on a bottle opener pulls off the bottle top.

5

Pushes and pulls

You push or pull on a lever to make it work. When you push or pull, the lever also makes a push or a pull. Scientists call all pushes and pulls "forces."

These are wire cutters. When you push on the handles, the blades cut through the wire.

On paper, arrows are used to show pushes and pulls. The arrow points in the direction of the pushing or pulling force. A longer arrow means a bigger push or pull.

This force arrow shows that this person's feet are pushing down on the ground.

Red arrows show pushes and pulls.

Blue arrows show movement.

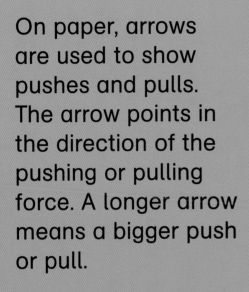

This girl is pushing down. The lever is pushing the rock up.

How a lever works

A lever is a long, narrow piece of material, such as a metal bar or a wooden stick.

A lever can make a push or a pull larger or smaller. It can also change the direction of a push or pull. The lever moves, or pivots, at a point that does not move, called the fulcrum.

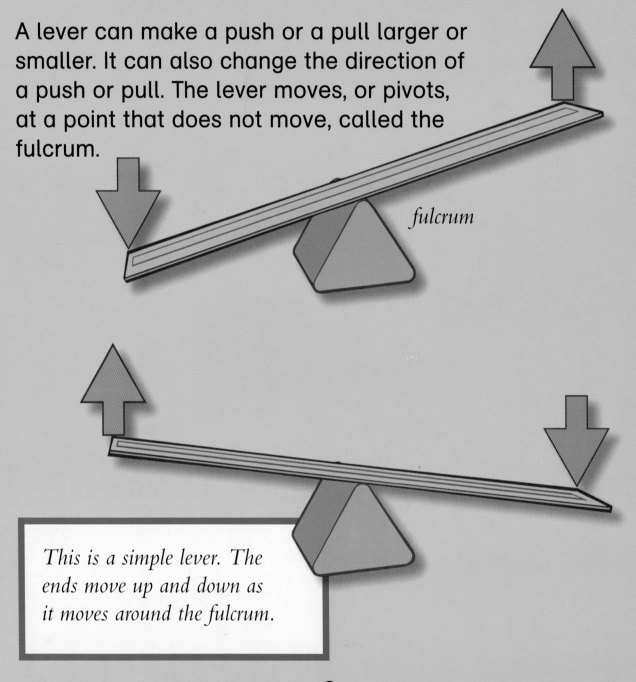

fulcrum

This is a simple lever. The ends move up and down as it moves around the fulcrum.

These levers make the men's pushes larger. The levers turn the bolts until they are tight.

These tweezers have two levers that are connected. They make a push smaller so you can pick up small things.

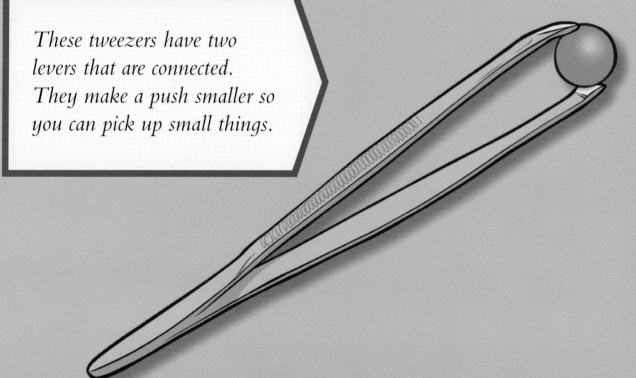

Lifting with levers

We use levers to help lift heavy things.

A crowbar is a long metal bar with bent ends. Crowbars lift concrete slabs or drain covers. A small push down on the crowbar lifts the heavy slab or cover.

A push down on the crowbar lifts the drain cover.

The flat, curved end of the crowbar fits under the edge of the drain cover.

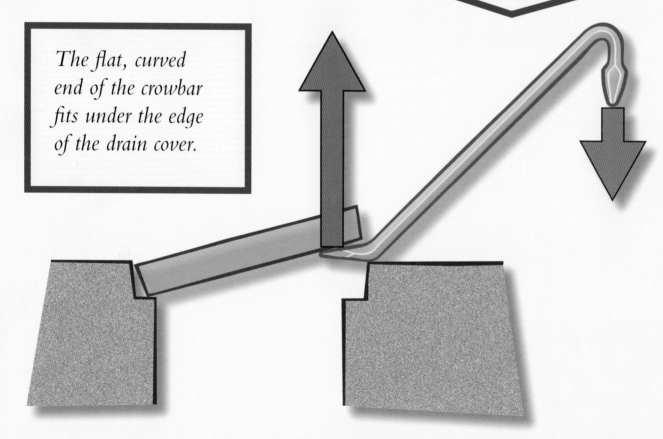

On a seesaw, the fulcrum is in the middle.

A seesaw is a lever. When you sit on one end of a seesaw, your weight pushes down on it. That pushes up the person at the other end.

A seesaw changes the direction of a push from down to up.

Turning with levers

We use levers to turn things. A wrench turns nuts and bolts.

A wrench's handle is a lever. The handle makes it easier to tighten nuts and bolts or to loosen them.

The wrench adjusts to fit the top of a nut or bolt.

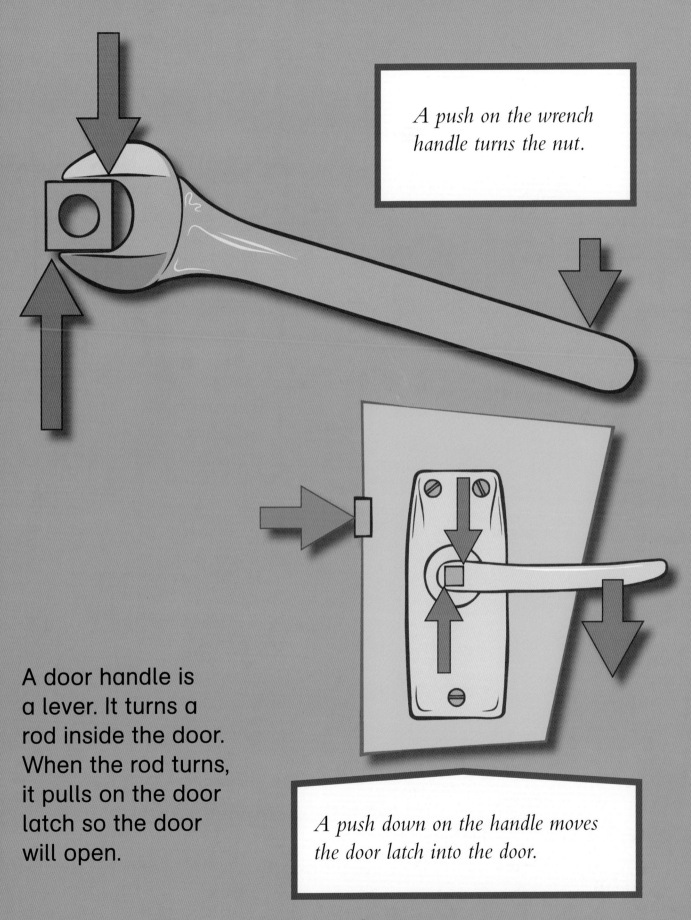

A push on the wrench handle turns the nut.

A door handle is a lever. It turns a rod inside the door. When the rod turns, it pulls on the door latch so the door will open.

A push down on the handle moves the door latch into the door.

Gripping with levers

**We use levers to grip things tightly.
A pliers is a gripping tool.**

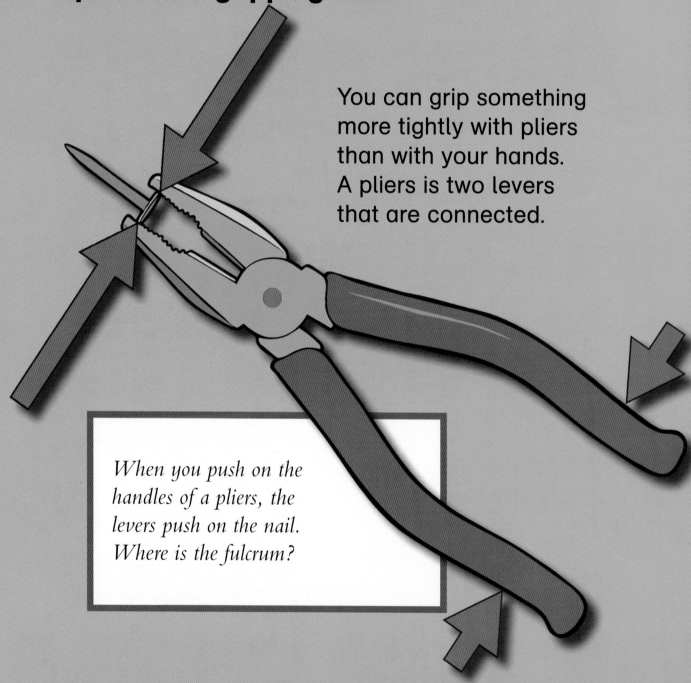

You can grip something
more tightly with pliers
than with your hands.
A pliers is two levers
that are connected.

*When you push on the
handles of a pliers, the
levers push on the nail.
Where is the fulcrum?*

> *The two levers in a pair of tongs are connected at one end.*

A pair of tongs is made of two connected handles. Each handle is a lever. Squeezing the two handles makes the ends of the levers move together to grip an object.

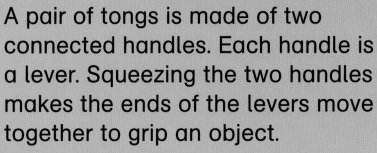

> *When you push on the handles, the jaws move together.*

Cutting with levers

We use levers to cut things. A paper cutter is a machine that cuts paper. Its handle and blade are a lever.

When the handle is pushed down, the lever makes the push bigger so the blade slices through the paper.

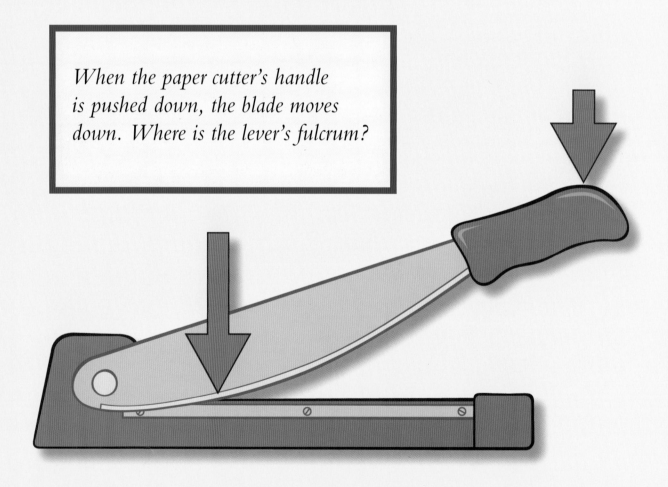

When the paper cutter's handle is pushed down, the blade moves down. Where is the lever's fulcrum?

A pair of bolt cutters is made of two handles joined together. Each handle is a lever. When the two handles are pushed together, the levers make a bigger push. This helps the blades cut through thick metal.

When the handles are pushed together, the blades move together.

Bolt cutters have long handles. This makes cutting metal easier.

Levers in machines

Complicated machines often use levers to work.

The brake handle on a bicycle is a lever. Pulling on the handle makes the handle pull a wire. The wire makes the brakes work.

A bicycle's brake handle is often called a brake lever.

Some exercise machines have levers. Pulling or pushing on the lever is hard work. Making the push or pull is good exercise.

Pushing and pulling these levers exercises the arms.

A sailor steers a sailboat with a rudder. The sailor moves the rudder from side to side with a lever called a tiller.

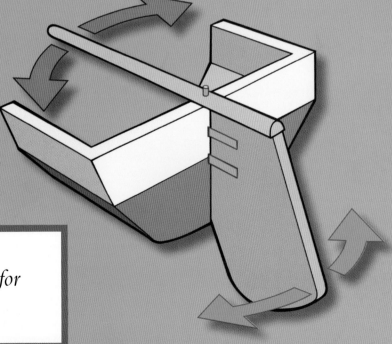

The tiller makes it easier for a sailor to steer a sailboat.

More levers in machines

Many building machines use levers to work. An excavator uses many levers.

This excavator's arm has two levers. Where are their fulcrums?

An excavator's arm is made of levers joined together. The levers are pushed and pulled by hydraulic pistons that make them move up and down. The pistons are like the muscles in your arm.

There are levers inside a tractor's cab. The driver pushes and pulls on the levers to make parts of the tractor work.

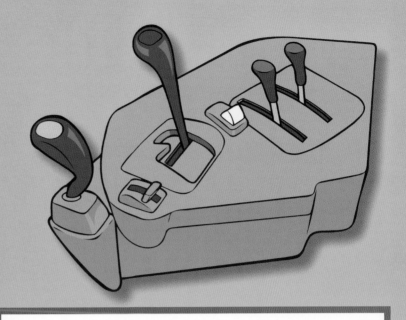

The levers help the driver work the heavy tractor with gentle pulls and pushes.

A scissor lift raises people and equipment up in the air. The platform is supported by many levers.

Why do you think this machine is called a scissor lift?

Levers in the past

People have been using levers for thousands of years.

The heavy baskets of stones pull down. This lifts up the water bucket.

This simple machine is called a shadoof. It lifts water from a stream to pour on crops in the fields.

Simple weighing machines use levers.
The object being weighed hangs on one
end and weights hang on the other end.

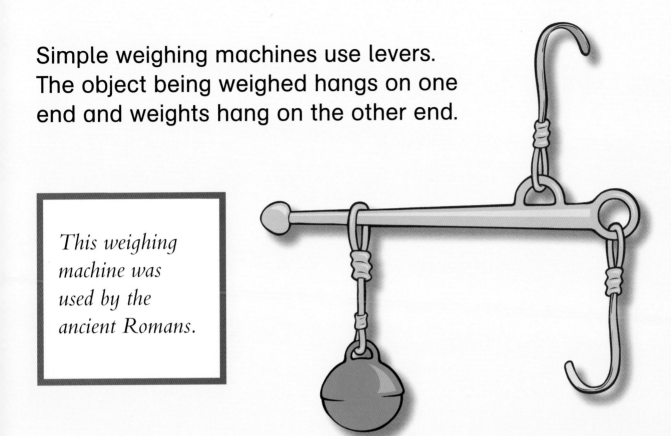

*This weighing
machine was
used by the
ancient Romans.*

Levers were even used in battle.
This machine is called a trebuchet
(treb-u-shay). It used a lever to
throw heavy rocks at an enemy.

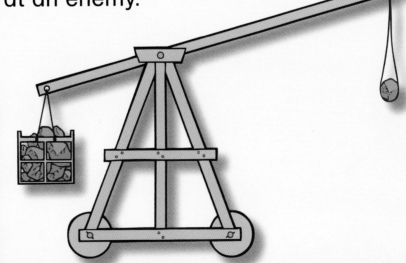

*The lever on a
trebuchet was
moved by a heavy
load of rocks.*

Fun with levers

The activities on the next four pages will help you understand how levers work.

A LIFTING LEVER

You will need:
• a plastic or wooden ruler 12 inches (30 cm) long
• a pencil
• modeling clay
• a small book

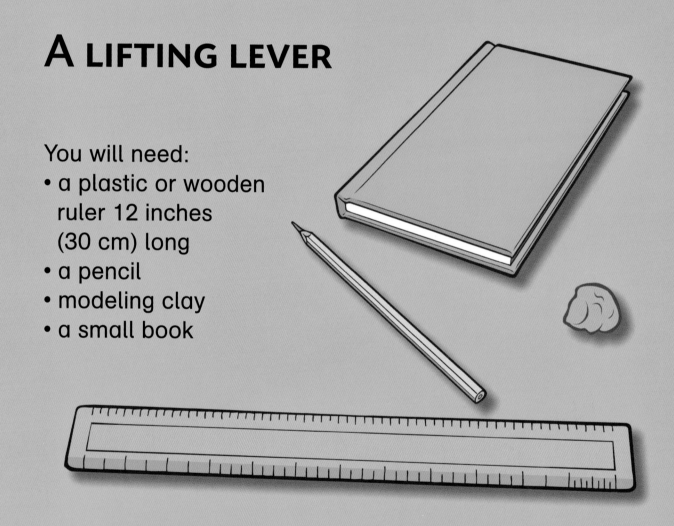

| 1 | Put the pencil on a table. Press a lump of modeling clay on each end to keep the pencil from moving. |

2 Place the ruler on the pencil so that the four-inch (10 cm) line is over the pencil.

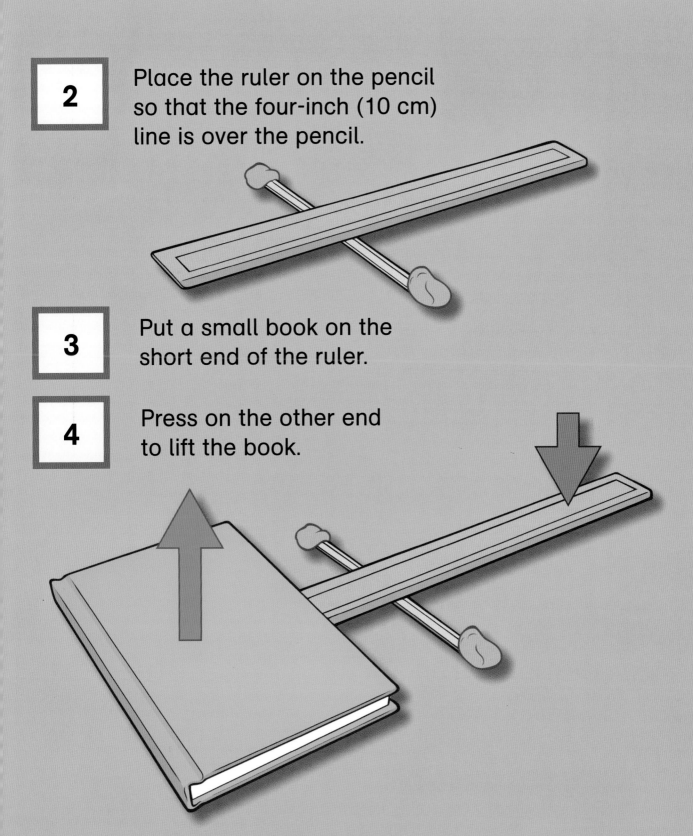

3 Put a small book on the short end of the ruler.

4 Press on the other end to lift the book.

The lever (ruler) makes your push bigger. It makes it easier to lift the book.

A BROOM LEVER

You will need:
- a broom (or a strong stick such as a broom handle)
- a large plastic box
- some books

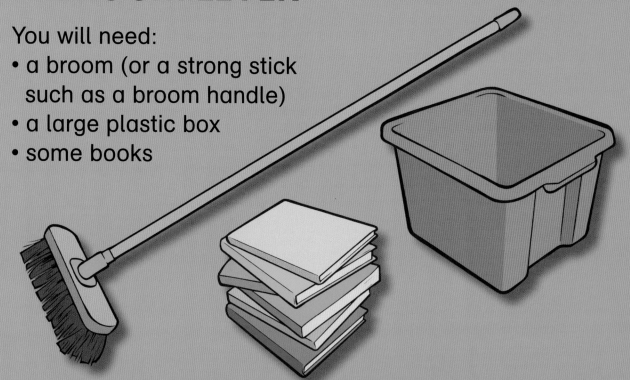

A gardener uses a shovel as a lever to pull up a potato plant.

1 Put the books in the box to make the box heavy.

2 Try pushing the box along the floor. Remember how hard you have to push to move the box.

3 Put the box against a wall. Place the end of the broom handle behind the box.

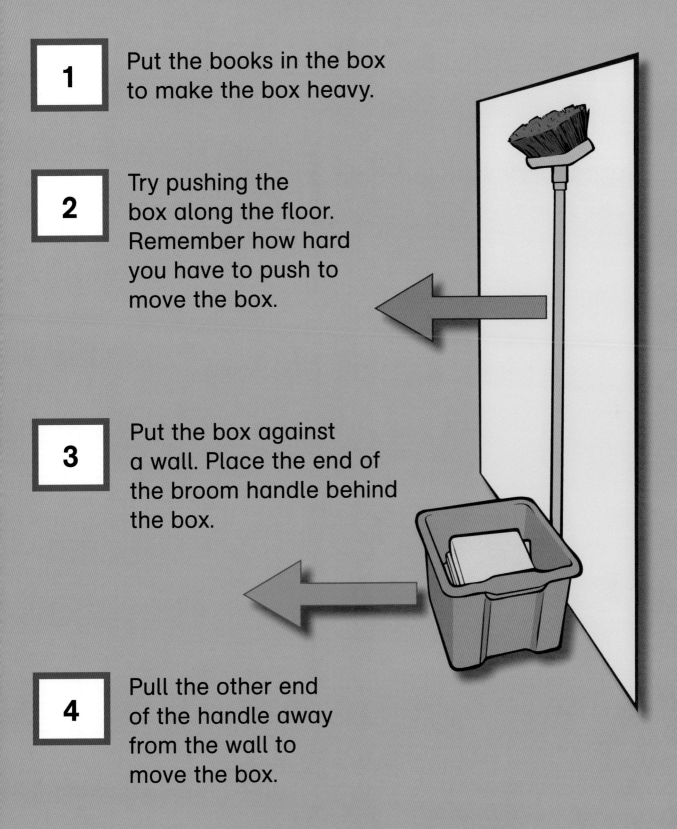

4 Pull the other end of the handle away from the wall to move the box.

The broom works like a lever. It makes it easier to move the box.

Find the lever

Can you find all the levers on these pages? Try to figure out what each lever does.

Which part of this wheelbarrow is a lever?

Where is the lever here? What job does it do?

Where do you pull on this lever? What does the lever pull on?

What is the lever here? What makes the lever move?

Answers are on page 32.

Words to remember

bolt cutters
A machine made of two levers,
used for cutting through thick bolts.

crowbar
A long, steel bar with bent ends.

forces
Pushes or pulls.

fulcrum
A nonmoving point that a lever pivots around.

paper cutter
A machine for cutting paper and card stock.

pliers
A simple machine made of two levers,
used for gripping things tightly.

rudder
A flat piece of material on the back of a sailboat.
It turns from side to side to steer the boat.

shadoof
A lever used to lift water from a well or a stream.

tiller
A lever used to turn the rudder of a sailboat
from side to side.

trebuchet
A simple machine used in the past by soldiers
to throw rocks at an enemy.

wire cutters
A machine made of two levers, used for cutting wire.

wrench
A lever used to turn a nut or bolt.

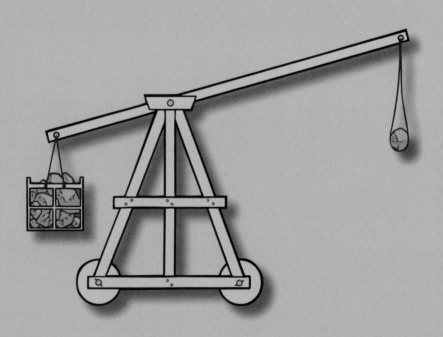

Index

Answers to pages 28–29

The long handles of a wheelbarrow are levers.
The red handle is a lever. Pulling it squeezes water from the sponge.
Pulling down on the hammer handle pulls out the nail.
Your arm is a lever! Your muscles move it.